PARIS FASHIONS OF THE 1890s

A Picture Source Book with 350 Designs, Including 24 in Full Color

Edited by
STELLA BLUM

DOVER PUBLICATIONS, INC.
New York

Published in Canada by General Publishing Company, Ltd., 30
Lesmill Road, Don Mills, Toronto, Ontario.
Published in the United Kingdom by Constable and Company, Ltd.

*Paris Fashions of the 1890s: A Picture Source Book with 350 Designs,
Including 24 in Full Color* is a new work, first published by Dover
Publications, Inc., in 1984.

Book design by Carol Belanger Grafton

Manufactured in the United States of America
Dover Publications, Inc., 31 East 2nd Street, Mineola, N.Y. 11501

Library of Congress Cataloging in Publication Data
Main entry under title:

Paris fashions of the 1890s.

1. Fashion—France—Paris—History—19th century—Pictorial
works.   I. Blum, Stella.
GT887.P27   1984   391′.2′0944361   83-5286
ISBN 0-486-24534-9

INTRODUCTION

When one compares the last decade of the nineteenth century with those it followed, it is easy to understand how it came to be called the "Gay Nineties." The fashions of the period reflect much of this spirit; by then there was a good measure of relaxation from the earlier rigid moral standards and stiff formal manners. A growing middle class started to fill in the previously almost unbridgeable gap between the privileged and the underprivileged. The Victorian view of the role of women solely as acquiescent wives and devoted mothers was on the wane, and women were now entering actively into areas once primarily the territory of men. The increasing number of newly made millionaires gave rise and credence to the Horatio Alger myth. In America, unfettered by strong traditions, it was possible to achieve positions of power and prominence simply by amassing great wealth. And because it became apparent that money could buy not only comfort and luxury, but also respect, the movement toward materialism, already in progress, was given strong impetus.

Expanding industrialization offered both work and the opportunity to make money. As though drawn by a magnet, the rural population was now gravitating toward the cities to make its fortune. This period marked not so much the end of a century as the beginning of a new one. To many people, bursting with energy and high hopes, the future looked full of promise. Railroads, telephones, bicycles, the new horseless carriages encouraged people to move, mingle and communicate more readily. Urbanization led them to cluster socially and to find entertainment away from home, at picnics, fairs, parks and at restaurants which started to flourish at all levels. Electricity, which could turn darkness into daylight, gave rise to more nightlife with a good deal of dancing and singing. The popular music had a lilting charm and an undeniably joyful gaiety.

By our standards life for most in the 1890s was far from easy—wages were low, hours were long and work was hard. But never before could so many people look to a life beyond basic subsistence. In spite of their harsh existence, they could hope to improve their lot and to find some time and money to pause for enjoyment. As a result, participation in fashion, once the prerogative of a privileged minority, became possible for all who were interested in it.

Although Paris was still the acknowledged leader of fashion, and the designs of the French couture were highly prized and proudly worn, there was a new spirit and determination with which the less affluent climbed aboard the fashion bandwagon. Taking their cue from what was being shown in Paris, they interpreted the fashion in terms of their own means and to suit their own tastes. Where fabrics such as handsome brocades, lush satins and velvets, exquisite silks and soft woolens were too expensive, readily available cheap imitations and less grand materials were used. To compensate for this lack of opulence, the scale of the silhouette was broadened and the colors heightened in intensity and contrast. The rich, in turn, not to be outshown by their "inferiors," picked up and further exaggerated the form of the silhouette. With their own status assured by the fineness of the fabric of their gowns and the richness of their trimmings, they not only accepted the preference for bright colors but also went on to promote the use of odd and even discordant combinations. In this carnival of shapes and hues, with its questionable sense of good taste, quality to some degree became of secondary importance. Fashion seemed mainly interested in projecting the robust exuberance of its participants.

Most of us are prone to round off periods of time into centuries, decades and the like, but fashion on its evolutionary path pays little heed to this system of marking changes. For example, in the 1890s, besides the main fashion—generally referred to as the "hourglass figure"—there was the end of an earlier cycle and the beginning of a new one locked in this ten-year bracket. The opening years of the decade showed a strong kinship to the fashions of the late 1880s. Bustles, though diminished, had not yet been discarded; skirts were still pulled back and bunched up over these contraptions to produce a rear hip extension. Compared to the silhouette that was to follow, this earlier fashion had an aura of restraint. Its aspect of containment and compactness is in strong contrast to the explosion and aggression one senses in the costumes of the mid-1890s, when shoulders jutted outward, skirts flared out and hats shot upward. By 1898, as though totally spent, fashions began to revert to the natural form, contenting themselves with merely expanding the curve of the bosom and the hips.

In spite of these differences, there was an evolving continuity, as there is generally in fashion, in the costumes of this period. One can detect the coming changes in the early part of the decade. Sleeves have begun to swell at the shoulders. The high-necked band, which was to increase in height and last for almost 20 years, can be seen on almost all women's clothes except evening gowns. Skirts had widened subtly from the knees down with the help of pleats, slits and flounces. The same confluence is true of the costumes of the last two or three years of the 1890s. While discarding the features of the preceding period, fashions gradually assumed those of the next era. Sleeves lost their fullness, skirts narrowed and took on a bell shape to merge into the smooth curvilinear silhouette of the turn of the century.

The publication of fashion plates began both in France and England in the late eighteenth century. By the end of the nineteenth century European and American ladies could choose from over a hundred publications which would tell them what to wear and how to look well dressed. Most of the plates in this book were originally published as supplements to a periodical titled *The Young Ladies' Journal*. It was first printed in the 1860s and ran into the early years of the twentieth century. Published in London, the magazine had its prints made in France. The fashions were labeled Parisian but since it was not unusual at this time for magazines to select, adapt or modify French designs to suit their readership, these plates were probably slanted to appeal to English and possibly even American women. The inclusion of children's fashions supports this theory, since most French fashion periodicals paid little heed to them.

Today the fashions of the nineties seem remote, even strange. Yet in many ways they parallel our current fashions. Both reflect an insistent departure from the past and express this breaking away in flamboyant statements. Growing out of their own times, however, each has produced its own very unique fashion image, each quite different from the other in spite of the similarity of the forces behind them.

PARIS FASHIONS
OF THE 1890s

WOMEN'S COSTUMES. a: Dinner gown of poppy red; bodice, sleeves and underskirt of black with gold dots; black feathers. **b:** Suit of steel gray with gold-braid trim. **c:** Dress of moss green striped and patterned in black. **d:** Suit of bright blue edged with white; rose-pink ribbon at neck.

EVENING AND DINNER GOWNS. a: Flesh pink with claret red. **b:** Almond green trimmed with olive green. **c:** Natural-colored sheer printed in green, lace edged; bodice and underskirt of crimson velvet. **d:** Lavender tunic printed in black over pale pink lavender. **e:** Light blue with white; black tie; pale yellow vest. **f:** Rose lavender striped in black; black lace and feather trimming.

VISITING COSTUMES. a: Dotted white; pale roses at neck and on hat. **b:** Powder blue with white lace. **c:** White with pattern and insets of pale lavender. **d:** Light willow green over white lace. **e:** Ivory with floral sprigs and hem of olive green; black lace-edged jacket. **f:** Old rose with white lace.

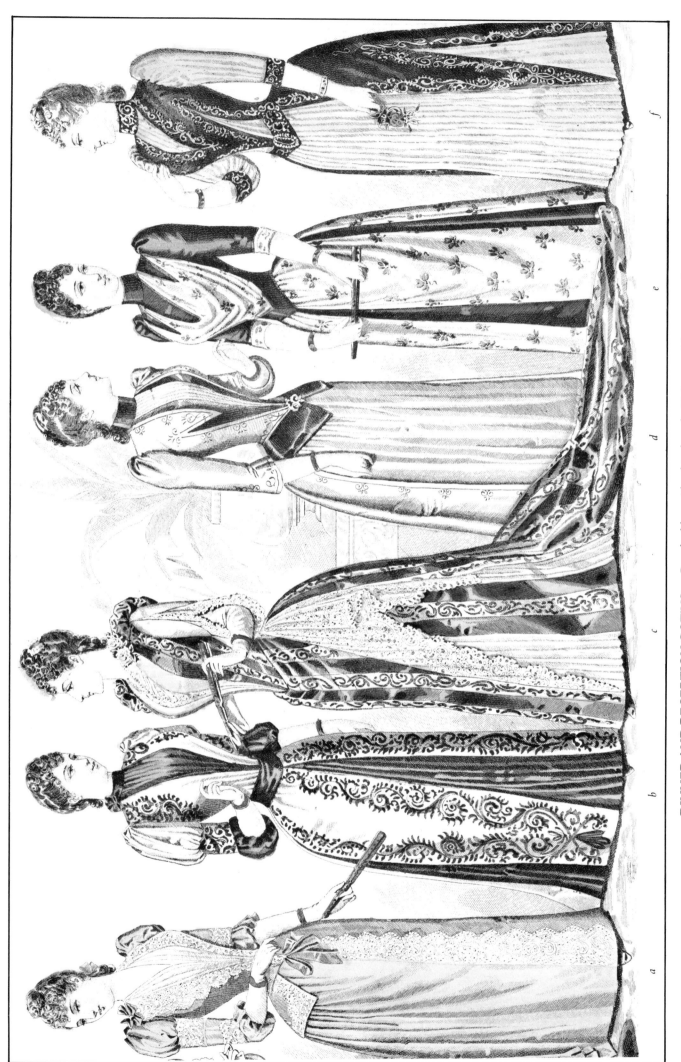

DINNER AND RECEPTION GOWNS. a: Powder blue with white lace. **b:** Light tan with pattern and underdress of tobacco brown. **c:** Rose pink patterned in black alternating with stripes of claret red; bodice, sleeve and skirt insets of rose pink; white lace trimming. **d:** Light gray; collar and bodice trim of black. **e:** Pale champagne with gray flowers; bodice and skirt insets of maroon. **f:** Bottle green over pleated pale aquamarine.

WOMEN'S COSTUMES. a: Suit of light gray; skirt front and lapels of medium gray trimmed with black braid. **b:** Evening gown of ivory silk with wild-rose print over white lace skirt; corsage and train of camellia pink. **c:** Afternoon costume of porcelain blue with rust brown. **d:** Dinner costume of sea-foam green and white floral stripes; white lace.

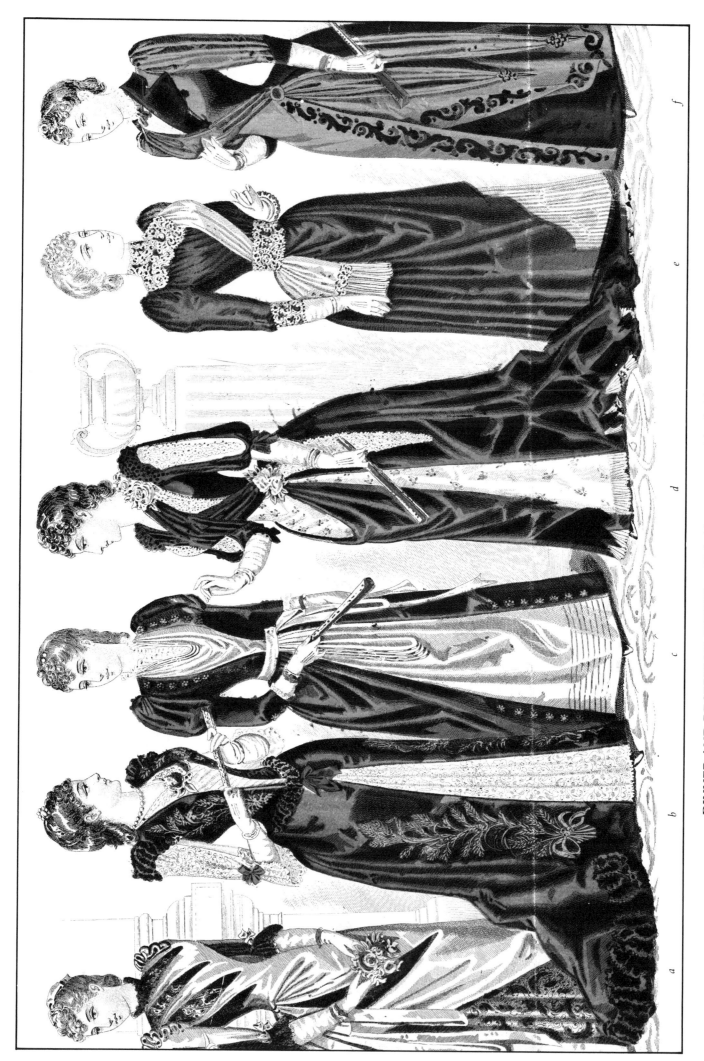

DINNER AND RECEPTION GOWNS. a: Light blue-gray over midnight blue. **b:** Blue-black with bronze embroidery; white lace; coral bows and flowers. **c:** Chrome-green redingote with bronze buttons; linden-green dress. **d:** Coral red over pale patterned pink. **e:** Navy blue with light blue. **f:** Burnished gold with russet brown.

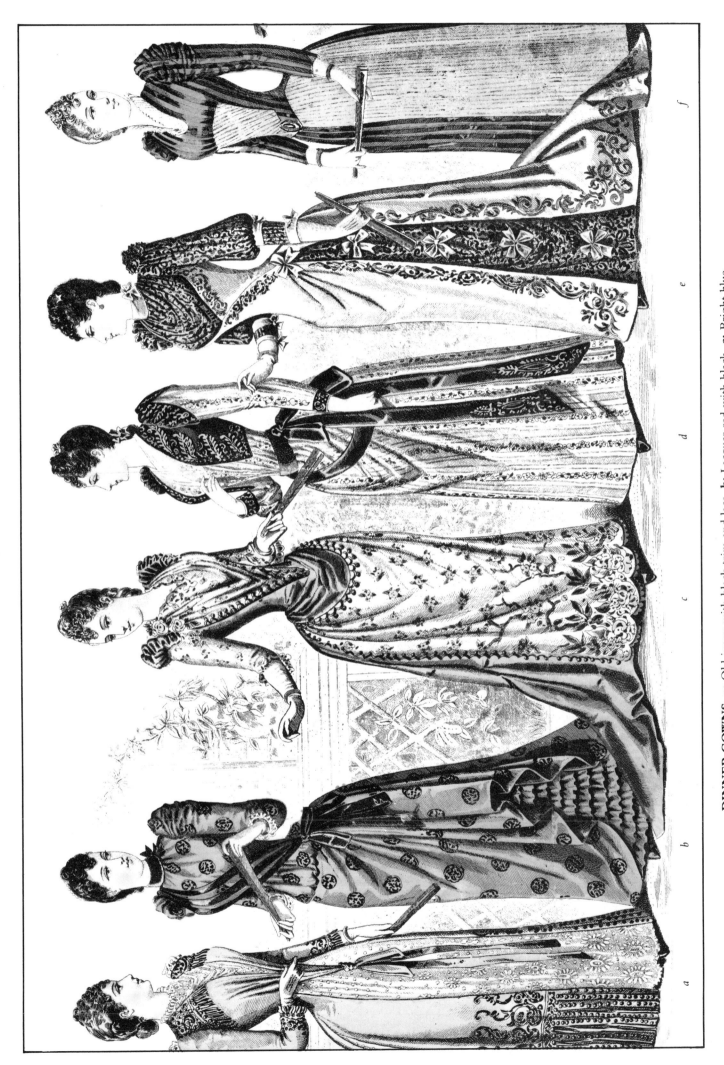

DINNER GOWNS. a: Old ivory with black trim and lace. **b:** Lacquer red with black. **c:** Bright blue polonaise over ivory. **d:** Ivory striped gown with peach flowers; rust-brown bolero; claret-red sash. **e:** Pale rose with black. **f:** Green and black stripes with pale blue-gray.

7

a   *b*   *c*

OUTDOOR COSTUMES. a: Pale pine green with black; pink parasol with white lace. **b:** Child's costume of champagne color with violet. **c:** Black lace-edged jacket; skirt of old rose with black stripes.

DAY AND DINNER COSTUMES. a: Yellow patterned in old gold; white lace and black feather trim. **b:** Powder blue with gold and fur trim. **c:** Tan with black. **d:** Vermilion with black stripes and lace. **e:** Cadet blue with black.

PROMENADE COSTUMES. a: Yellow and white stripes; white lace. **b:** Orchid with white lace; yellow flowers. **c:** Bamboo-colored costume. **d:** Pink pearl with white lace. **e:** Orchid stripes with bands of yellow floral sprigs on ivory; orchid at neck, on sleeves, waist, hem and parasol. **f:** Powder blue and white lace.

OUTDOOR COSTUMES. a: Slate blue with black braid. **b:** Tunic jacket of wheat color with bronze trim; gray skirt with blue stripes. **c:** Oyster-white coat; skirt crossbarred in red and black. **d:** Black braid and lace-trimmed wrap; cherry-red skirt striped in black. **e:** Light gray trimmed with gunmetal; white skirt and vest. **f:** Black mantle; black, green and red striped skirt.

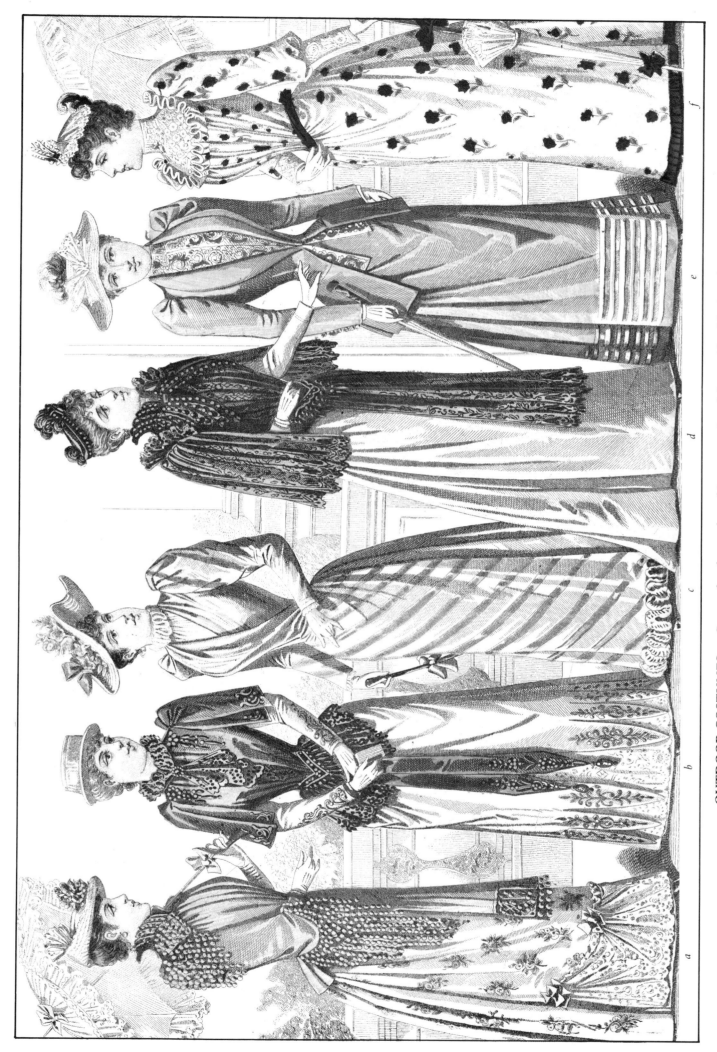

OUTDOOR COSTUMES. a: Putty-colored mantelet; white, rose-sprigged dress with white lace. **b:** Black jacket; pale blue dress with white lace underskirt. **c:** Shell pink with lavender stripes. **d:** Black jacket; pale aquamarine dress. **e:** Straw color with white and bronze. **f:** Ivory with carnation-red print.

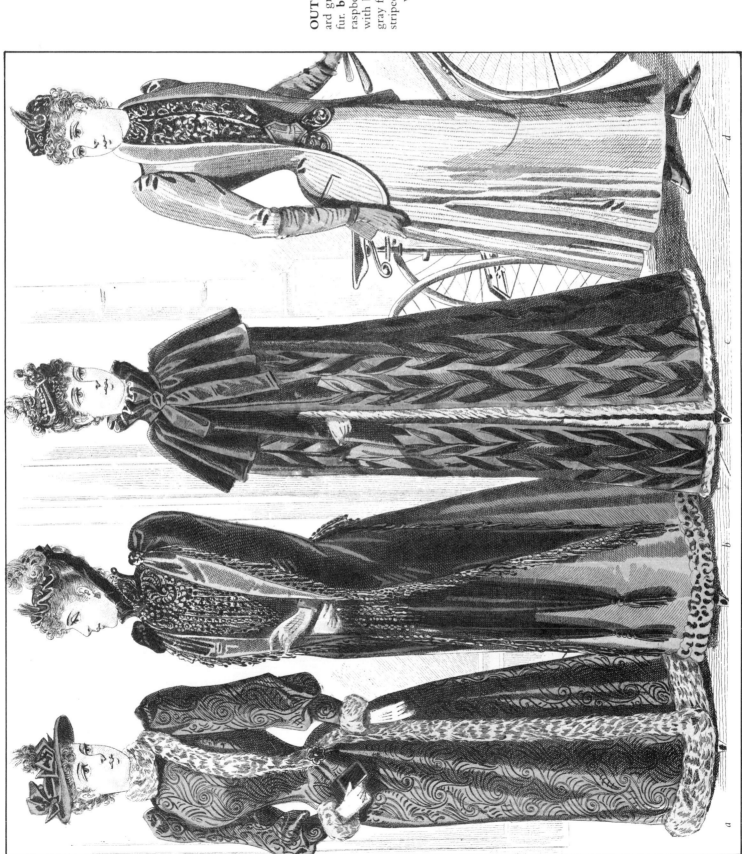

OUTDOOR COSTUMES. a: Lizard green with black braid and gray fur. **b:** Black mantelet; dress of pale raspberry red. **c:** Cape of nut brown with bottle-brown pattern; lining of gray fur. **d:** Bicycle suit of gray, pin-striped in black; black braid-trimmed vest; fawn gloves and belt.

DINNER COSTUMES. a: Gray with brown fur over white with black braid trim. **b:** Pink and white stripe with white lace. **c:** Mauve pink with black. **d:** Fawn with yellow gold and white lace. **e:** Blue–gray with white lace. **f:** Tunic jacket of chrome green; pale green dress.

OUTDOOR COSTUMES. a: Black jacket; costume of apple green striped with hunter green. **b:** Jacket of fawn with brown sleeves, braid trim and fur; skirt of pale raspberry. **c:** Steel-gray coat with black braid. **d:** Teal-blue patterned velvet with light brown fur. **e:** Rust-colored jacket with black braid trim; off-white skirt crossbarred in black.

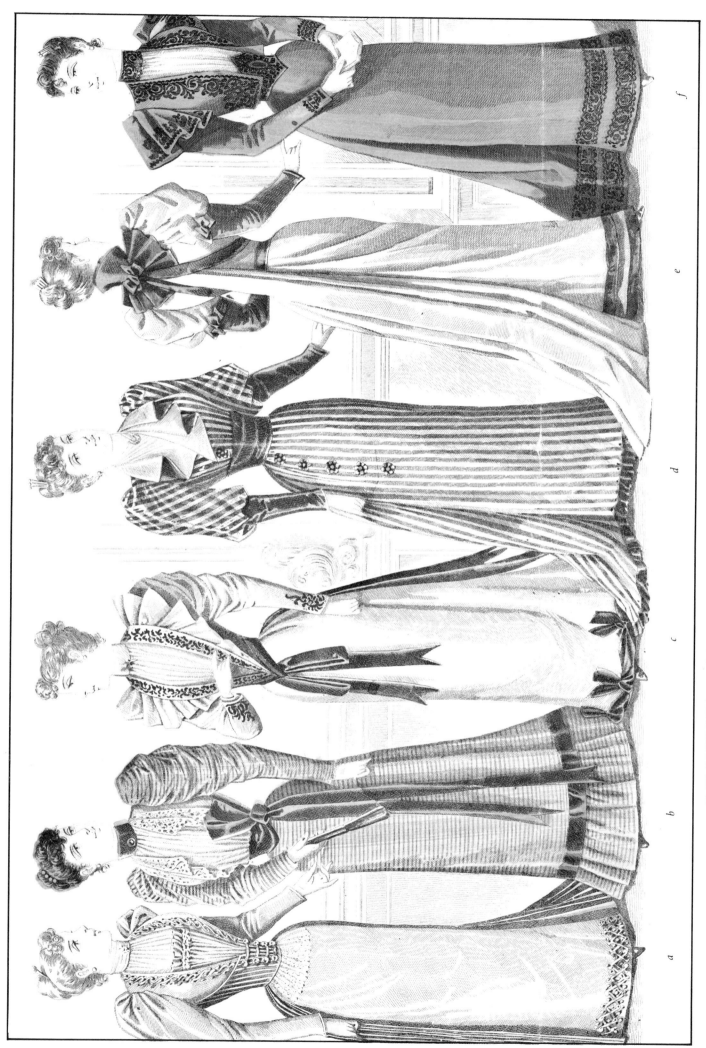

DAY COSTUMES: **a:** Pale lavender; orchid and black stripes; white lace. **b:** Beige striped with brown; brown ribbon; white lace trim. **c:** Green–gray with black; pink vestee. **d:** Pink striped and trimmed with black. **e:** Gray with black. **f:** Cherry with black; white blouse.

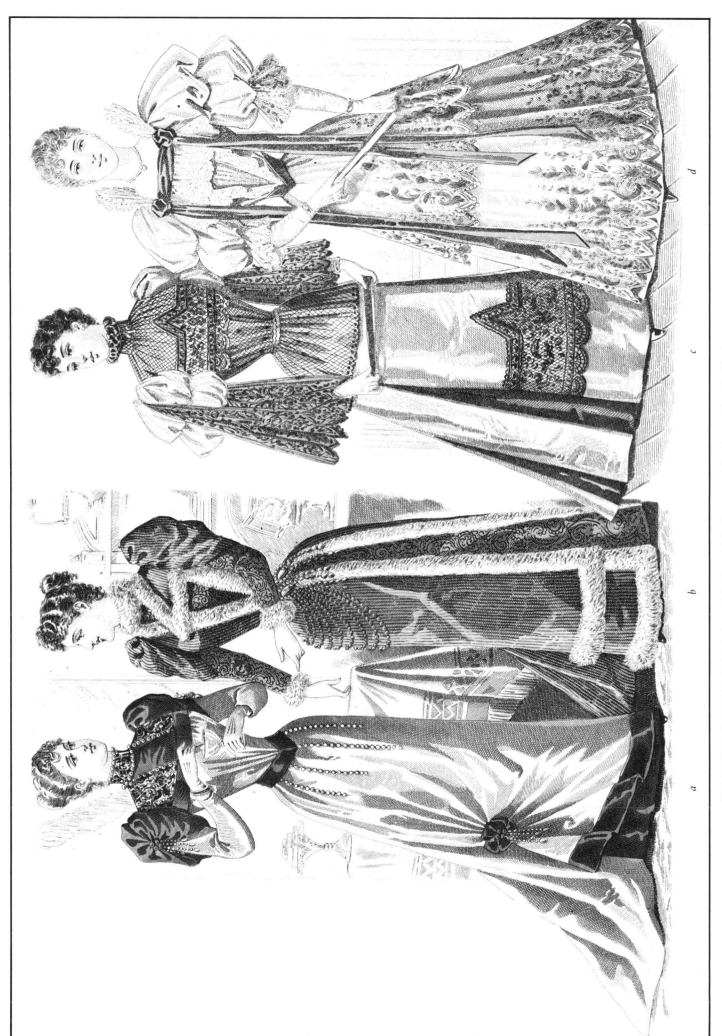

WOMEN'S COSTUMES (1/93). a: Pale lime with olive green. **b:** Gray striped in black over terra-cotta patterned in black; light gray fur trim. **c:** Iridescent brass; black lace. **d:** Lavender with purple.

AFTERNOON DRESSES. a: Pink with ivory lace; neck and waist accents of apple green. **b:** Pale green striped in gray; forest green at neck and waist; white lace. **c:** Periwinkle blue with hyacinth; white lace. **d:** Beige with white lace; blue vestee, lapel edging and hat trim. **e:** White with lemon-yellow flowers and ribbons.

WINTER WEAR. a: Long black cape with brown fur; dahlia-mauve with black braid trim. **b:** Lacquer-red coat trimmed with black over skirt of iridescent green-to-red silk. **c:** Nut-brown coat trimmed with gray fur. **d:** Black coat with gray fur. **e:** Teal-blue coat with brown fur.

a   *b*

WOMEN'S COSTUMES (10/95). a: Suit of pale amber with white; rose trim on hat. **b:** Fur-trimmed
black cape over dress of moss green striped in emerald green and black.

a *b*

EVENING GOWNS (10/95). a: Iridescent silk, pale green to pink; floral pattern in camellia pink. **b:**
Powder-blue skirt; dark blue bodice with white lace; pale yellow sleeves and bodice trim; pale pink roses.

CHILDREN'S COSTUMES (10/95). a: Cobalt-blue costume; red and white bodice; beige cape facing and spats. **b:** Boy's costume of white shirt, brown pants, black shoes and stockings. **c:** Girl's costume: bodice of pale yellow with dark blue; skirt of striped porcelain blue. **d:** Dress of light periwinkle blue. **e:** Garnet dress; beige jacket with white lapels. **f:** Cinnamon-colored suit; black lapels and high shoes; pale pink blouse with white lace.

a

b

WOMEN'S COSTUMES (10/95). a: Suit of periwinkle blue; vest and hat trim of cherry red. **b:** Shooting costume of terra-cotta wool crossbarred in brick red and tan; yoke, cuffs and hem of tan; spats and hat of gray.

23

WOMEN'S COSTUMES (11/95). a: Gown of oyster white over powder blue; royal-blue ribbons; white lace. **b:** Suit of light cedar brown with brown fur. **c:** Teagown of lime green with salmon; white lace.

DAY DRESSES (11/95). a: Powder blue with blouse of pale yellow patterned in olive green. **b:** Terra-cotta with pale rose sleeveless jacket trimmed with brown fur.

OUTDOOR COSTUMES (11/95). a: Coat of bright camellia with gray fur. **b:** Suit of medium gray over golden yellow.

OUTDOOR COSTUMES.

EVENING GOWNS (11/95).

CHILDREN'S COSTUMES (2/96).

DAYTIME COSTUMES (3/96).

LADIES' COSTUMES (5/96).

SUMMER GOWNS (8/96).

PROMENADE COSTUMES (9/96).

SUMMER COSTUMES (6/99).

WOMEN'S COATS (11/95). a: Pale blue with gray fur; red skirt and hat. **b:** Bright green with light brown fur.

CHILDREN'S COSTUMES (11/95). a: Pale blue with red sash. **b:** Pea-green coat; hat with red trim and green feathers. **c:** Boy's suit of pale beige. **d:** Coat of red with black bands and gray fur. **e:** Coat of bright blue with bronze bow and hat trim.

WOMEN'S COSTUMES (11/95). a: Champagne-colored coat with royal blue; pale blue lining. **b:** Tunic
jacket of powder blue. **c:** Nile green with cuffs and bretelles of claret red.

WOMEN'S COSTUMES (1/96). a: Ball gown of powder blue with pink flowers and Dresden-blue bows.
b: Day dress of light coral wool; pale yellow sleeves; black ribbons and facings. **c:** Evening gown of bright
pink with white lace; sleeves of scarlet.

CHILDREN'S COSTUMES (1/96). a: Clear light blue with ivory ties and bows; garnet yoke, cuffs and spats. **b:** Champagne with forest green. **c:** Willow green with hunter green. **d:** Leaf green with black. **e:** Lavender trimmed and patterned in garnet red. **f:** Light gray coat; black fur and high shoes; hat with red feathers.

DAY AND EVENING COSTUMES (2/96). a: Day dress of nut-brown tweed; underdress spring green
with raspberry-red print. **b:** Ball gown of Nile blue with red floral sprigs; green ribbon trim; blue pink roses
on corsage.

DAY COSTUMES (2/96). a: Ivory-white skirt; champagne bodice with blue-violet cuffs and bretelles. **b:** Pale rose gray with rust-red blouse and hem. **c:** Royal blue with white lace and brown fur. **d:** Pea green with forest green. **e:** Vermilion with royal blue. **f:** Biscuit color with black fur; red accent in hat.

CHILDREN'S COSTUMES (3/96). a: Light rose with royal blue. **b:** Blue-gray with garnet. **c:** Fern green with black. **d:** Pale apricot with lavender. **e:** Pea green with strawberry.

WOMEN'S COSTUMES (3/96). a: Fawn with terra-cotta; brown collar, cuffs and belt. **b:** Blue-gray with raspberry-red ribbons. **c:** Pale blue skirt; sand-colored cape with dark brown fur and blue flowers.

COSTUMES (3/96). a: Child's dress of powder pink with scarlet rosettes. **b:** Evening cape of lavender over ivory gown. **c:** Day dress of aquamarine blue with white; brown fur trim. **d:** Girl's dress of bois de rose with dark green.

WOMEN'S SUITS (4/96). a: Pale blue tweed with black; rose at neck and on hat. **b:** Lavender tweed with black; yellow vestee.

DAY COSTUMES (5/96). a: Black lace with ivory yoke; light blue gown. **b:** Powder-pink dress with mahogany-red bow and cuffs. **c:** Melon-pink coat with black braid; cherry-red hat ribbon. **d:** Lavender suit with oyster white.

DAY COSTUMES (5/96). a: Dress of apricot with bright pink belt, neck bow and hat trim. **b:** Suit of sea-foam green with ivory cuffs, revers and vest; white blouse with rose-red bow and hat flowers.

39

CHILDREN'S COSTUMES (5/96). a: Porcelain blue with white lace and apricot trim. **b:** Apricot with white yoke and maroon ribbons at neck, on skirt and on hat. **c:** White with bottle green. **d:** Rose pink with light blue and white lace. **e:** Aquamarine dress; ivory jacket.

DAY COSTUMES (5/96). a: Striped blue-gray suit with pink cuffs and lapels; hat with caramel-colored ribbon and red feathers. **b:** Dress of ivory patterned in black; purple velvet belt and neckline details; pale green collar and neckline inset.

DAY COSTUMES (6/96). a: Powder blue with pink flowers; white lace sleeve and wrist trim; champagne vestee and revers; rose accents on hat. **b:** Champagne skirt; forest-green jacket with lime-green sleeves with tan floral patterns; white gold-trimmed lapels.

SUMMER DRESSES (6/96). a: Sea-foam skirt and blouse; spring-green jacket and hat trim. **b:** Pale blue, gold edged, striped with bright blue, over white.

CHILDREN'S COSTUMES (6/96). a: Ashes of roses with crimson ribbons. **b:** Bright blue with white.
c: Caramel color with lavender waist inset. **d:** White with bottle green. **e:** Very pale green with light blue
around neck and sleeves; teal-blue ribbon belt.

SUMMER COSTUMES (7/96). a: Tennis dress of ivory striped in lavender; lavender collar, vestee, cuffs, belt and hat trim. **b:** Suit of gray with rust brown; white vest-blouse.

45

DAY DRESSES (7/96). a: Powder blue with white; pea-green tulle on hat. **b:** Ivory with green; bois-de-rose bodice, belt and hat flowers. **c:** Pearl gray with white spots; bright green cuffs, hat trim; rose-pink collar and hat ties.

CHILDREN'S CLOTHES (7/96). a: Light blue patterned in black; white yoke. **b:** Straw color with leaf green. **c:** Pale green with geranium-red belt and hat trim. **d:** Champagne iridescent silk; lavender apron with blue ribbons. **e:** Ivory dress; apricot belt; cherry-red ribbon on hat.

47

CHILDREN'S COSTUMES (9/96). a: Powder blue with white. **b:** Natural-straw hat with green ribbons. **c:** Coat of iridescent champagne color with white yoke; green ribbon trim. **d:** Champagne dress trimmed with Prussian blue. **e:** Pale green with dark olive green; white lace yoke. **f:** Purple beret. **g:** Lavender dress; white lace yoke and sleeve trim; copper-brown belt.

VISITING DRESSES (9/96). a: Pale blue-gray with neck, waist, hat and skirt trim in raisin color. **b:** Shell
pink with black.

AFTERNOON COSTUMES (10/96). a: Blue-gray patterned silk; bodice and sleeve ruffles of orchid pink; black lapels, cuffs and skirt trim. **b:** Aquamarine green; purple velvet bolero; bodice of white crossbarred with blue and pink.

OUTERWEAR (10/96). a: Coat of light amber trimmed with black. **b:** Pale pink cape with white lace; bright green dress. **c:** Gray with black bands; pale pink lapels with red trim; garnet-red hat.

51

OUTDOOR COSTUMES (10/96). a: Jacket of Vandyke brown with oyster-white revers; light green blouse, crossbarred in red and dark green; skirt of striped lavender; green bows in hat. **b:** Suit of biscuit-colored wool; Capri-blue hat trim.

WOMEN'S COSTUMES (11/96). a: Day costume of coral with gray fur. **b:** Evening gown of powder blue with white spotted stripes; cherry-red and pink bodice and skirt trim.

53

WOMEN'S COSTUMES (11/96). a: Pale blue with burgundy. **b:** Light willow green with brown fur;
cerise bow in hat. **c:** Aquamarine gown with white lace.

CHILDREN'S COSTUMES (11/96). a: Hyacinth trimmed with picot-edged jade-green ribbons. **b:** Tan straw hat with hunter green. **c:** Sea-foam green with garnet-red belt. **d:** Fawn-colored suit with garnet belt and hat ribbon. **e:** Strawberry-red dress with black. **f:** Como blue with navy and brown fur trim. **g:** Black hat with raspberry-red ribbon and beige feathers.

EVENING GOWNS (12/96). a: Lime green with gold dots; white bodice, emerald-green sash and trim. **b:**
Pale amethyst; white bodice; rust-brown belt.

BALL GOWNS (12/96). a: White with lavender stripes; bodice of pale lavender chiffon with purple, green and gold; sash of deep purple. **b:** Pale yellow striped and trimmed with light blue; sash belt of deep blue. **c:** Green patterned in gold edged with red flowers; white inset; pale yellow sleeves, bodice and hem trim.

DAY COSTUMES (1/97). a: Coral tweed with short bolero of white with gold; China-rose vest; emerald-green necktie and bow. **b:** Heather tweed with emerald-green bodice; white neck bow. **c:** Iridescent silk, light blue to copper brown; black lapels.

DAY AND EVENING GOWNS (1/97). a: Ball gown of pink striped in brick red; orange with yellow
around bodice top. **b:** Dress of Pacific blue trimmed with gray fur; white-with-gold neckline inset. **c:** Gown
of black lace over pale yellow striped in purple; purple at waist.

CHILDREN'S COSTUMES (1/97). a: Vermilion coat. **b:** Black hat with medium blue ribbon and red feathers. **c:** Beige coat with light brown fur. **d:** Porcelain blue, gray fur; cardinal-red collar and belt. **e:** Apricot with black. **f:** Gray hat with bright red. **g:** Aquamarine green with white fur.

a   b   c

WOMEN'S AND CHILD'S COSTUMES (2/97). a: Suit of gray with black. **b:** Cream jacket with gray fur; light blue dress and hat feathers; garnet belt and hatband. **c:** Suit of biscuit color with cream bands.

BALL GOWNS (2/97). a: Lime with white lace and lavender ribbons; jade-green flowers at neckline. **b:** Turquoise blue with white lace; blond flowers; bright coral ribbon. **c:** Rose pink; emerald-green bodice with white lapels.

AFTERNOON AND EVENING GOWNS (1/97). a: Pale green with white. **b:** Powder pink with pale
yellow; white and black vestee. **c:** Pale lavender; white blouse; black tie and sash.

WOMAN'S AND CHILDREN'S COSTUMES (2/97). a: Coat of clay color with gray fur. **b:** Suit of light blue with white collar and lapels. **c:** A party dress of pale lavender with white bodice and yellow ribbon trim. **d:** Suit of Nile green with brown fur. **e:** Party dress of light yellow with scarlet.

DAY COSTUMES (5/98). a: Powder blue with pale yellow. **b:** Pale peach with apricot bands. **c:** Lavender gray with light blue.

SUMMER DRESSES (5/98). a: Lilac gray with white lace. **b:** Gray-green with white; lavender belt.

OUTDOOR COSTUMES (5/98). a: Bottle-green jacket with pale yellow; gray skirt. **b:** Copper with oyster white. **c:** Sea-foam green with white.

LATE SPRING COSTUMES (5/98). a: Pale green and white. **b:** Lavender blue with white lace. **c:** Pale yellow, white lace; black belt.

DAY COSTUMES (5/98). a: Pale green and white. **b:** Lavender gray; fern green on jacket fronts; white blouse. **c:** Gray-green with white lace; brown belt.

SUMMER COSTUMES (6/98). a: Muted apricot with white lace edged with brown. **b:** Gray-green with black-and-white revers; coral vest, tie and hat trim.

VISITING COSTUMES (7/98). a: Apple green with white lace. **b:** Wisteria with white lace. **c:** White with green leaves; burnt-umber belt, tie and hat trim.

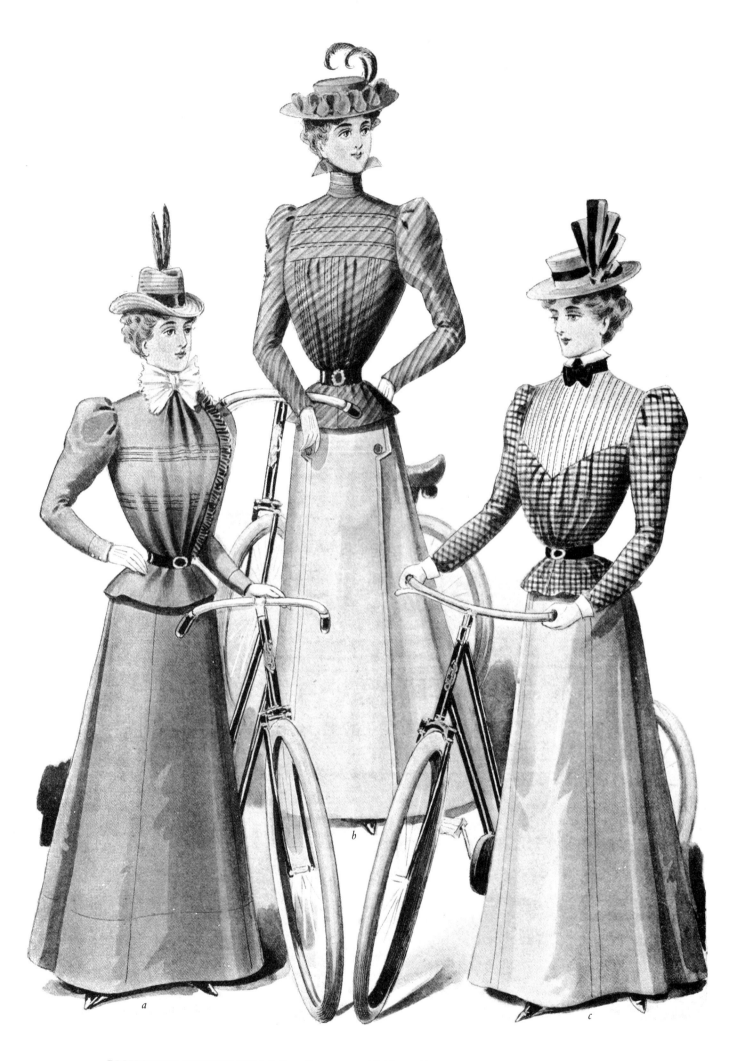

BICYCLING COSTUMES (7/98). a: Dove gray with blue ruffle and white tie. **b:** Heather blouse striped in light blue; oyster-white skirt; black belt. **c:** Pale lime blouse, checked in green; pale yellow yoke; burnt-sienna tie; brown belt; pearl-gray skirt.

AFTERNOON COSTUMES (7/98). a: Iris gray with off-white lace. **b:** Porcelain green trimmed with pale rose; pink roses on hat and pink parasol with white. **c:** Ivory striped in shell pink; cedar-brown hat, bows and buttons.

AUTUMN COSTUMES (9/98). a: Blue orchid trimmed with brown fur; caramel-colored blouse. **b:** Olive brown; lilac blouse and jacket revers; white-feather collar. **c:** Mauve gray with almond-green bow appliqués, belt and hat trim; white-lace bow and cuffs; pink rose in hair.

VISITING COSTUMES (9/98). a: Tan silk with black and lacquer red; red hat with blue birds' wings. **b:** Rose gray with teal-blue bands; collar, lapels and belt of juniper green. **c:** Mauve-taupe with white lace; palmetto green on hat.

WINTER COSTUMES (1/99). a: Juniper green with black fur; brown satin ribbon around waist. **b:** Medium blue with ecru lace; maroon tie and belt.

WINTER COSTUMES (1/99). a: Cloud blue with black fur and bands; hat trimmed with brown ribbon.
b: Almond green with white revers; navy-blue blouse. **c:** Rose-glow tan with white; cinnamon-colored blouse.

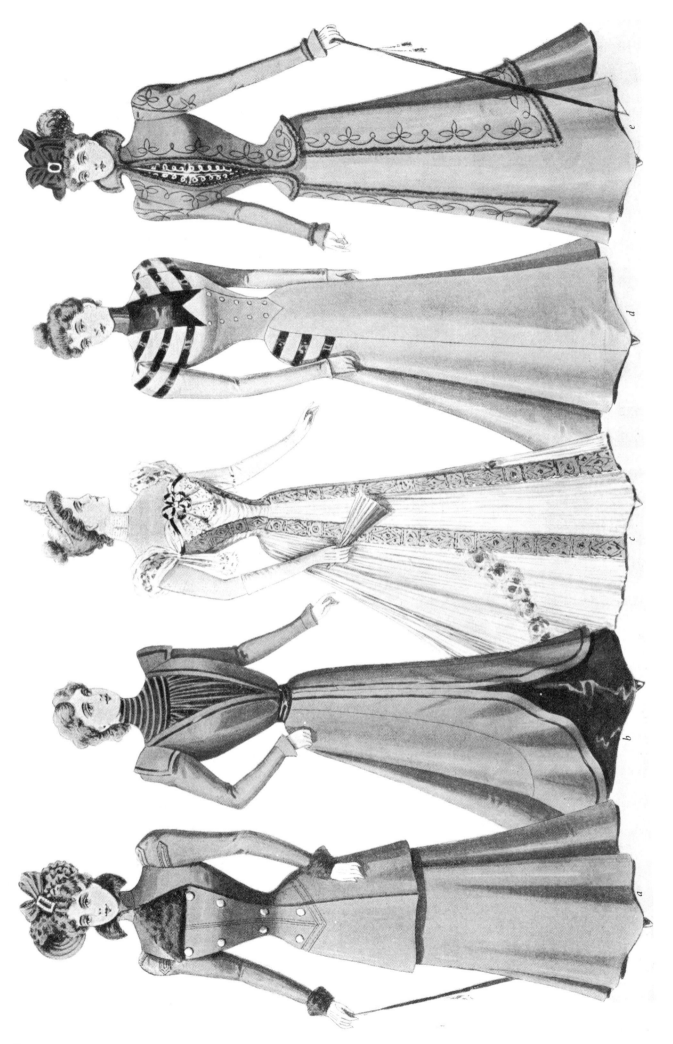

DAY AND EVENING COSTUMES (1/99). a: Blue orchid with brown fur. **b:** Light chestnut brown with midnight blue. **c:** White with coral bands and yellow flowers. **d:** Light blue with blue-black. **e:** Apricot with brown fur; black vestee; coral ribbon on hat.

DAY AND EVENING COSTUMES (2/99). **a:** Powder blue with white. **b:** Mauve-gray with white. **c:** Light green with forest green, white bodice, inset and trim. **d:** Mauve-gray; pearl gray striped in mauve. **e:** Nutmeg brown with brown fur; lapels and cuffs of bronze green.

79

OUTDOOR COSTUMES (2/99). a: Gunmetal gray; white skirt; black tie. **b:** Slate gray with brown fur;
maroon ribbon on hat.

WOMEN'S COSTUMES (3/99). a: Clay color with orange appliqués; gray feathers at neck; brown lapels.
b: Almond green; lime-green top; brown-ribbon trim. **c:** Light raisin brown; top and underskirt of pink lavender; white lace at neckline.

WOMEN'S SUITS (3/99). a: Metal gray with white blouse; rose vest. **b:** Strawberry with white lapels and blouse.

WOMEN'S COSTUMES (3/99). a: Orchid brown with cedar brown. **b:** Green-gray with gunmetal. **c:**
Orchid brown; teal-blue feathers on hat.

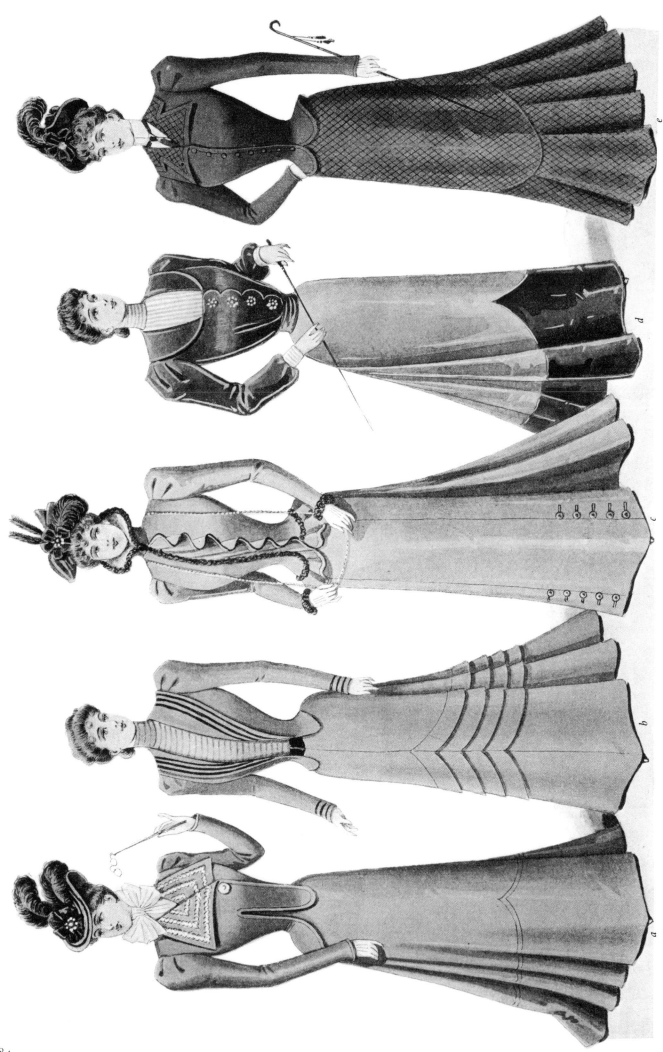

DAY COSTUMES (3/99). a: Lavender-gray with white. **b:** Rose tan; pale blue lavender. **c:** Cloud blue with black. **d:** Almond green with hunter green; white blouse. **e:** Cedar brown; white skirt; black tie.

OUTDOOR COSTUMES (5/99). a: Powder blue with white braid; pink blouse with black. **b:** Tan with white braid and black bands. **c:** Pale aquamarine with white braid. **d:** Light lavender with white. **e:** Maroon with black bands; white collar, yellow blouse.

85

WOMEN'S COSTUMES (5/99). a: Coral pink with white. **b:** Vandyke brown with white and rose
passementerie. **c:** Gray with white stripes; white shirt; black tie; black-and-white parasol.

a　　　　　　　　　　　　　　　　　　　*b*

SPRING SUITS (5/99). a: Tan with light blue lapels, belt and parasol. **b:** Claret red, crossbarred in rust red; black braid trim; white blouse and vest; black tie.

VISITING COSTUMES (6/99). a: Pale rose with floral sprigs of coral; white lace; black ribbon trim. **b:** Blue lavender; pale blue bodice top with white patterning. **c:** Violet patterned in white and purple; bodice top and underskirt of amethyst.